MY DOG MATTIS

By Mark Tappan and Libby Hempen

ILLUSTRATED BY

Brittney Hassinger

PAPERBACK ISBN: 978-0-578-89174-3

THIS IS MY DOG MATTIS.

MATTIS IS DIFFERENT THAN SOME DOGS
BECAUSE HE HAS A JOB.

I EVEN HAD TO GO TO A SPECIAL SCHOOL TO GET HIM.

The school taught him all the things he would need to know to be a police dog.

There were a lot of dogs, but
Mattis was my favorite.
He always tried hard and never gave up!

He jumped

    really high

AND RAN VERY FAST.

He loved to chase the ball.

He also loved playing hide-and-seek with the ball, but he would use his NOSE to find it.

His nose smells things we can't smell.

He found the ball every time!

Heel!

HE LISTENED CLOSE

down!

AND WAS GREAT

Highfive!

AT FOLLOWING
DIRECTIONS.

I PICKED MATTIS OUT OF ALL THE OTHER DOGS BECAUSE I KNEW HE WAS GOING TO BE SPECIAL AND A GREAT FRIEND.

When he came to work with me, he did great!

He saved lost children.

He found hidden things with his nose.

AND HE HELPED CATCH BAD GUYS. MOST OF THE TIME THEY JUST GAVE UP WHEN THEY SAW HIM.

ONE DAY, SOME BAD GUYS DID NOT GIVE UP. THEY RAN AND MATTIS CHASED AFTER THEM.

THEY JUMPED OVER A WALL AND MATTIS JUMPED, TOO. THE WALL WAS VERY HIGH AND HE LANDED RIGHT ON THEM.

THE BAD GUYS FINALLY GAVE UP.

I WAS SO PROUD
OF MATTIS,

BUT WHEN I SAW HIM I
KNEW HE WAS HURT.

I KNEW I HAD TO GET HIM TO THE DOCTOR AS FAST AS I COULD.
I EVEN TURNED ON THE SIREN AND LIGHTS
ON MY POLICE CAR.

THE DOCTORS AT THE ANIMAL HOSPITAL
SAVED HIS LIFE.

I WAS SO GLAD
HE WAS GOING TO BE
OK,

BUT I DIDN'T KNOW IF HE

WOULD BE WELL ENOUGH

TO GO BACK TO

WORK WITH ME

But he got
better
every day!

OTHER PEOPLE HEARD HOW BRAVE HE WAS AND
HE GOT SPECIAL AWARDS FOR IT!

After one month, he was able to be back at work and we were both very happy!

A TV SHOW HEARD ABOUT MATTIS AND HIS BRAVERY AND THEY ASKED US TO BE ON THEIR SHOW.

WE WERE SO EXCITED BECAUSE MATTIS WOULD JUMP, SWIM, AND USE HIS NOSE TO COMPETE AGAINST OTHER DOGS.

We said yes!

ALL THE WAY TO CALIFORNIA.

ON THE SHOW, MATTIS

JUMPED,

SNIFFED,

AND SWAM.

HE HAD SO MUCH FUN AND...

My dog Mattis is my

BEST

FRIEND.

Thanks to
Tamara, Makenna, Cayden, and Harper.
I hope we make you proud.
Also to Mattis, Storm, and Hawk for the adventures!